TOP 10 C

TRAVEL GUI_ _υ23

Unveiling the Top 10 Hidden Gems, Iconic Sights, and Unforgettable Experiences

Linda J. Moore

INTRODUCTION TO CORSICA

Welcome To Corsica

Jean had always dreamt of visiting Corsica, the enchanting island nestled in the Mediterranean Sea. With its rugged mountains, picturesque beaches, and rich cultural heritage, Corsica had always held a special place in his heart. Finally, after years of longing, Jean's dream was about to come true.

As the plane descended towards the Ajaccio Airport, Jean's excitement soared. The breathtaking view of the island's jagged coastline and azure waters left him in awe. Stepping off the plane, he was greeted by a warm Mediterranean breeze, carrying the scents of wildflowers and sea salt.

Jean had meticulously planned his itinerary, eager to explore every nook and cranny of the island. He rented a car and embarked on a journey that promised to be filled with unforgettable adventures.

The first stop on his Corsican adventure was the capital city of Ajaccio. Jean wandered through the narrow streets, lined with colorful houses and quaint cafes. He immersed himself in the city's rich history,

visiting the birthplace of Napoleon Bonaparte and marveling at the intricate architecture of the Cathédrale Notre-Dame-de-l'Assomption.

Leaving Ajaccio behind, Jean ventured into the rugged interior of the island, where he discovered the true essence of Corsica. He hiked through the stunning mountain trails of the Parc Naturel Régional de Corse, surrounded by dense forests, cascading waterfalls, and the songs of birds echoing in the air.

In the charming village of Corte, Jean learned about Corsica's unique cultural heritage. He explored the ancient citadel, witnessing the remnants of a tumultuous past. The locals welcomed him with open arms, sharing stories of their ancestors and their unwavering pride in their Corsican identity.

Jean couldn't resist the allure of Corsica's pristine beaches. He spent lazy afternoons basking in the sun and swimming in the crystal-clear waters of Palombaggia and Santa Giulia. The vibrant marine life mesmerized him as he snorkeled through underwater caves and coral reefs.

As Jean's visit to Corsica came to an end, he couldn't help but feel a profound sense of gratitude. The island had exceeded all his expectations, captivating him with its natural beauty, fascinating history, and warm hospitality.

Corsica had left an indelible mark on Jean's soul, and he knew that he would forever cherish the memories of his visit. As he bid farewell to the island, he promised himself that one day, he would return to Corsica, to immerse himself once again in its irresistible charm and allure.

History and Culture

Corsica has a rich and turbulent history that has been shaped by its strategic location in the Mediterranean Sea. The island has been occupied by a succession of different cultures, including the Greeks, Romans, Carthaginians, Byzantines, Arabs, Genoese, and French.

The earliest evidence of human occupation on

Corsica dates back to the 3rd millennium BC. The island's first major civilization was the Torrean culture, which flourished from the 2nd millennium BC to the 7th century BC. The Torreans were a seafaring people who built fortified villages and traded with other cultures in the Mediterranean.

In the 6th century BC, the Greeks founded the colony of Alalia on the east coast of Corsica. The Greeks were followed by the Romans, who conquered the island in 259 BC. Corsica remained under Roman rule for over 500 years, during which

time the island's economy and culture flourished.

After the fall of the Roman Empire, Corsica was ruled by a succession of different powers, including the Byzantines, Arabs, and Genoese. The Genoese ruled Corsica for over 500 years, during which time they built many of the island's castles and fortifications.

In 1768, Corsica was sold to France by the Republic of Genoa. The French rule of Corsica was met with resistance from many Corsicans, who wanted independence for their island. The Corsican independence movement was led by Pasquale Paoli, who established a provisional government on the island in 1755.

The Corsican independence movement was eventually defeated by the French in 1769, but the island's culture and identity remained strong. Corsica became an integral part of France in 1815, but the Corsican language and culture continue to thrive today.

Corsica is a land of great natural beauty and cultural heritage. The island is home to a variety of historical sites, including ancient ruins, medieval castles, and Renaissance churches. Corsica is also known for its beautiful beaches, stunning mountains, and lush forests.

The Corsican people are known for their strong sense of identity and their love of their island. The Corsican language is a distinct Romance language that is closely related to Italian. Corsican culture is a blend of Mediterranean and Celtic influences, and it is characterized by its strong sense of community and its love of music and dance.

Geography and Climate

The geography of Corsica is dominated by mountains, which cover two-thirds of the island. The highest peak is Monte Cinto, which rises to 2,706 meters (8,880 feet). The mountains are divided into two main ranges, the Corsican Alps in the north and the Monte Renoso Massif in the south.

The climate of Corsica is Mediterranean, with hot, dry summers and mild, rainy winters. The average temperature in July is 22°C (72°F), while the average temperature in January is 8°C (46°F). The island receives an average of 35 inches (880 mm) of precipitation per year.

The coastline of Corsica is 1,000 kilometers (620 miles) long and is characterized by a variety of features, including cliffs, coves, and beaches. The most popular beaches on the island include Palombaggia, Santa Giulia, and Rondinara.

The climate of Corsica
varies with altitude. The
mountains are cooler and
wetter than the coastal areas.
The highest peaks can
experience snow in winter.
The vegetation of Corsica is
varied, reflecting the
different climates and
altitudes on the island. The
coastal areas are dominated
by evergreen trees, such as
pines, cypresses, and holm
oaks. The mountains are
home to a variety of
deciduous trees, as well as
shrubs and grasses.

GETTING TO CORSICA

Best Time to visit Corsica

- High season is from June to August, when the weather is warm and sunny, and the beaches are crowded. This is the best time to visit if you want to swim, sunbathe, and enjoy the island's many water sports. However, it's also the most expensive time to visit, and the island can be quite crowded.

- ** shoulder season** is from May to June and September to October. The weather is still warm and sunny, but the crowds are smaller and the prices are lower. This is a great time to visit if you want to enjoy the island's beauty without the crowds.

- Low season is from November to March. The weather is cooler, but it's still possible to enjoy the beaches and the outdoors. This is a great time to visit if you're looking for a more affordable and peaceful vacation.

If you're planning on hiking, the best time to visit is from May to September. The trails are less crowded and the weather is mild. However, if you're looking for a challenge, you can hike the GR20, a long-distance trail that crosses the island from north to south. The best time to hike the GR20 is from June to September.

By Air

The quickest way to get to Corsica is by plane. There are four airports on the island: Bastia Poretta Airport, Calvi Sainte Catherine Airport, Ajaccio Campo dell'Oro Airport, and Figari Sud-Corse Airport.

Airlines that fly to Corsica

- There are a number of airlines that fly to Corsica, including Air Corsica, EasyJet,

British Airways, and Ryanair. The most popular routes are from Paris, Nice, Marseille, and London.

Flight prices

- Flight prices to Corsica vary depending on the time of year, the airline, and the route. In general, you can expect to pay between €50 and €200 for a return flight.

Other expenses

- In addition to the cost of the flight, you will also need to factor in the cost of baggage, airport taxes, and transportation to and from the airport. Baggage fees vary by airline, but you can expect to pay around €20 for a checked bag. Airport taxes are typically around €10 per person. And transportation to and from the airport can cost around €20 per person.

Total expenses

- The total cost of a trip to Corsica by air will vary depending on your travel dates, the length of your stay, and your budget. However, you can expect to spend between €200 and €500 for a weekend trip, and between €500 and €1,000 for a week-long trip.

By Ferry

There are several ferry companies that offer ferries to Corsica, including Corsica Ferries, Moby Lines, and La Méridionale. The most popular ferry routes are from Italy, France, and Sardinia.

Ferry routes from Italy to Corsica

- The most popular ferry routes from Italy to Corsica are from Livorno, Savona, and Nice. The ferries from Livorno are the fastest, with a crossing time of just over 2 hours. The ferries from Savona and Nice take a little longer, with crossing times of around 3 hours.

Ferry routes from France to Corsica

- There are also several ferry routes from France to Corsica, including from Toulon, Marseille, and Bastia. The ferries from Toulon and Marseille take around 4 hours to reach Corsica. The ferries from Bastia are the fastest, with a crossing time of just over 1 hour.

Ferry routes from Sardinia to Corsica

- There are also a few ferry routes from Sardinia to Corsica, including from Santa Teresa di Gallura, Porto Torres, and Golfo Aranci. The ferries from Santa Teresa di Gallura are the fastest, with a crossing time of just over 50 minutes. The ferries from Porto Torres and Golfo Aranci take around 1 hour to reach Corsica.

Ferry expenses

- The cost of a ferry ticket to Corsica varies depending on the route, the time of year, and the type of ticket you purchase. However, you can expect to pay between €50 and €200 for a one-way ferry ticket.

ACCOMMODATION IN CORSICA

Hotels and Resorts

- Location: Olmeto, Corsica
- Amenities: Sea-view rooms and suites, fine-dining restaurant, spa, infinity pool

Hôtel Cala di Greco

- Average daily expenses: €250-€350
- Location: Bonifacio, Corsica
- Amenities: Modern suites with patios, infinity pool, bar, sea-view sundeck

Grand Hôtel Cala Rossa & Spa NUCCA

Hôtel Marinca & Spa

- Average daily expenses: €300-€400

- Average daily expenses: €400-€500
- Location: Lecci, Corsica

- Amenities: Airy rooms, tree house, spa, elegant restaurant, private beach

Guesthouses and Bed & Breakfasts

Castellu d'Orezza: Castellu d'Orezza is a charming guesthouse located in the heart of the Corsican mountains. It is a former 18th-century fortress that has been converted into a luxurious bed & breakfast. The guesthouse offers stunning views of the surrounding countryside, and it is just a short walk from the village of Carcheto-Brustico.

The guesthouse has 6 bedrooms, all of which are

beautifully decorated and have private bathrooms. The guesthouse also has a swimming pool, a sauna, and a Jacuzzi. Guests can enjoy a delicious breakfast each morning, which is made with fresh, local ingredients. Price: Doubles start from €120 per night.

Châtelet de Campo: Châtelet de Campo is a stunning bed & breakfast located in the village of Campo. The guesthouse is set in a beautiful stone building that dates back to the 17th century. It is surrounded by lush gardens and has stunning views of the surrounding mountains.

The guesthouse has 5 bedrooms, all of which are beautifully decorated and have private bathrooms. The guesthouse also has a swimming pool, a terrace, and a garden. Guests can enjoy a delicious breakfast each morning, which is made with fresh, local ingredients. Price: Doubles start from €100 per night.

Casa del Sole: Casa del Sole is a lovely guesthouse located in the village of Sari-Solenzara. The guesthouse is set in a beautiful Mediterranean garden and has stunning views of the surrounding mountains and sea. The guesthouse has 4 bedrooms, all of which are beautifully decorated and have private bathrooms. The guesthouse also has a swimming pool, a terrace, and a garden. Guests can enjoy a delicious breakfast each morning, which is made with fresh, local ingredients. Price: Doubles start from €80 per night.

CORSICA'S NATURAL WONDERS

Scandola Nature Reserve

The Scandola Nature Reserve was established in 1975 to protect its unique natural beauty and biodiversity. The reserve covers an area of 19.19 square kilometers, of which 9.19 square kilometers is land and 10 square kilometers is sea. The reserve is home to over 1,200 plant species, including many endemic species that are found nowhere else in the world. The marine life in the reserve is also very diverse, and includes dolphins, seals, seabirds, and fish.

The Scandola Nature Reserve can only be visited by boat. There are several boat tour operators that offer trips to the reserve, and most of them depart from the town of Porto. The boat tours typically last for several hours, and they allow visitors to see the stunning scenery of the reserve from up close.

Some of the highlights of a boat tour to the Scandola Nature Reserve include:

- Seeing the dramatic volcanic coastline, with its towering cliffs, caves, and arches.
- Watching the seabirds soaring overhead, including cormorants, shearwaters, and gannets.
- Spotting dolphins and seals swimming in the crystal-clear waters.
- Visiting the tiny village of Girolata, which is only accessible by boat or on foot.

Bavella Massif

The Bavella Massif is a popular destination for hikers, climbers, and nature lovers. There are a variety of trails to choose from, ranging from easy walks to challenging climbs. The massif is also home to a number of caves and canyons, which can be explored by experienced spelunkers.

One of the most popular attractions in the Bavella Massif is the Col de Bavella, a high mountain pass that offers stunning views of the surrounding peaks. The pass is also home to a number of restaurants and shops, making it a convenient place to stop for refreshments or souvenirs.

Another popular destination in the Bavella Massif is the Aiguilles de Bavella, a group of seven granite needles that rise up from the surrounding forest. The needles are a popular spot for climbers, and there are a number of routes to choose from, ranging from easy to difficult.

Restonica Valley

The Restonica River flows through the valley, carving out a series of deep gorges. The gorges are lined with pine and birch forests, and the river is home to a variety of fish, including trout and salmon. The valley is also home to a number of endemic plant species, including the Corsican hellebore.

The Restonica Valley is a popular destination for hikers, and there are a number of trails to choose from, ranging from easy walks to challenging hikes. The most popular hike is the one to Lac de Melo and Lac de Capitello, which takes about 2 hours to complete. The hike is strenuous in some places, but the views from the lakes are well worth the effort.

In addition to hiking, the Restonica Valley is also a popular destination for swimming, picnicking, and fishing. There are a number of spots along the river where you can swim in the cool, clear water. There are also a number of picnic areas along the river, where you can enjoy a meal with stunning views of the mountains.

Lavezzi Islands

The archipelago is located about 4 kilometers (2 miles) from the Corsican mainland, 7 km (4 mi) from Cape Pertusato, and 10 km (6 mi)

southeast of Bonifacio. It covers 5,123 ha in area and the highest point is 50 metres (164 feet). They include the southernmost point of Metropolitan France. The two main islands are Cavallo (112 ha), the only inhabited island in the archipelago, and Lavezzu (Italian: Lavezzo, 66 ha), just on the south of Cavallo. The other islands or islets are, from west to east: Piana, Ratino, Porraggia and Sperduto (or Perduto).

The Lavezzi Islands are a popular tourist destination, known for their beautiful beaches, turquoise waters, and dramatic scenery. The islands are also a protected nature reserve, home to a variety of plants and animals, including seabirds, dolphins, and seals.

There are a few ways to get to the Lavezzi Islands. The easiest way is to take a boat from Bonifacio. There are several companies that offer boat tours to the islands, and the journey takes about 30 minutes. You can also rent a boat and explore the islands at your own pace.

Once you're on the islands, there are plenty of things to do. You can swim, snorkel, sunbathe, hike, or simply relax on one of the many beautiful beaches. There are also a few restaurants and bars on the islands, where you can enjoy a meal or a drink with stunning views of the surrounding sea.

Corsican Regional Nature Parks

World Heritage Site in 1983. The reserve is home to a stunning array of cliffs, coves, and islets, as well as a variety of marine life, including dolphins, seals, and seabirds.

Another popular park is the Lavezzi Archipelago Nature Reserve, which is located off the coast of Bonifacio. The reserve is known for its white-sand beaches, clear waters, and lush vegetation.

One of the most popular Corsican Regional Nature Parks is the Scandola Nature Reserve, which was designated a UNESCO

In addition to these two popular parks, there are a number of other Corsican Regional Nature Parks that are worth exploring. These include the Nature Park of Cape Corse and Agriate, the Nature Reserve of the Strait of Bonifacio, and the Nature Reserve of Etang de Biguglia.

The Corsican Regional Nature Parks offer a variety of activities for visitors, including hiking, biking, camping, fishing, and boating. There are also a number of museums and visitor centers located in the parks, which provide information about the natural and cultural heritage of the region.

If you are looking for a place to experience the beauty and diversity of Corsica, then the Corsican Regional Nature Parks are a great option. With their stunning scenery, rich wildlife, and variety of activities, the parks offer something for everyone.

Here are some additional facts about the Corsican Regional Nature Parks:

- The parks are home to over 1,500 plant species, including many endemic species.
- The parks are also home to a variety of animal species, including the Corsican mouflon, the bearded vulture, and the river trout.
- The parks are a popular destination for hikers, bikers, campers, fishermen, and boaters.
- There are a number of museums and visitor centers located in the parks, which provide information about the natural and cultural heritage of the region.

Aiguilles de Bavella

The Aiguilles de Bavella are located about 50 kilometers (31 miles) north of Porto-Vecchio and 10 kilometers (6.2 miles) south of Zonza. The easiest way to reach the Aiguilles de Bavella is by car. The D268 road from

Zonza to Solenzara passes through the heart of the massif. There is a large parking area at the Col de Bavella, which is the starting point for most hikes and climbs in the area.

There are a variety of hiking trails in the Aiguilles de Bavella, ranging from easy to challenging. The Sentier des Douaniers is a popular easy hike that follows the ridgeline of the massif. The GR20 is a long-distance hiking trail that passes through the Aiguilles de Bavella.

The Aiguilles de Bavella are also a popular destination for climbers. There are many different climbing routes in the area, ranging from easy to difficult. The most popular climbing routes are located on the Pointe des Eboulis and the Punta di a Vacca.

Corsican Beaches

powdery, the water is clear and turquoise, and the views of the surrounding mountains are stunning. Palombaggia Beach is located in the south of Corsica, near the town of Porto-Vecchio.

- **Palombaggia Beach:** This is one of the most popular beaches in Corsica, and it's easy to see why. The white sand is soft and

- **Santa Giulia Beach:** This is another beautiful beach in the south of Corsica. It's smaller than Palombaggia Beach, but it's just as beautiful. The sand is white and fine, the water is clear and blue, and there are pine trees behind the beach for shade. Santa Giulia Beach is located near the town of Porto-Vecchio.

- **Saleccia Beach:** This is a secluded beach located in the Désert des Agriates, a natural park in the north of Corsica. The beach is surrounded by sand dunes and pine trees, and the water is a clear turquoise color. Saleccia Beach is a great place to relax and enjoy the peace and quiet

- Loto Beach: This is another secluded beach located in the Désert des Agriates. The beach is even more remote than Saleccia Beach, and it's only accessible by foot or boat. The sand is white and fine, the water is a clear turquoise color, and the views of the surrounding mountains are stunning. Loto Beach is a great place to get away from the crowds and enjoy the beauty of nature.

GR20 Hiking Trail

The GR20 is a long-distance hiking trail that crosses the island of Corsica diagonally, from Calenzana in the north to Conca in the south. The 180-kilometer (112-mile) trail follows the granite backbone of mountains that divide the island in two, many of which soar above 2,000 meters (6,600 feet) in altitude.

The GR20 is considered one of the toughest long-distance hikes in Europe, and is not for the faint of heart. The trail is steep and strenuous, with daily ascents and descents of up to 1,000 meters (3,300 feet). The terrain is also rugged and unpredictable, with loose rocks, scree slopes, and narrow ridges.

Despite its difficulty, the GR20 is also one of the most rewarding hikes in the world. The scenery is stunning, with breathtaking views of the Corsican mountains, forests, and coastline. The trail also passes through a variety of different microclimates, from the lush forests of the north to the arid plateaus of the south.

Hiking the GR20 is an unforgettable experience, but it is important to be prepared. Hikers should be in good physical condition and have a high level of fitness. They should also be experienced in backpacking and hiking in mountainous terrain.

The best time to hike the GR20 is during the summer months, when the weather is warm and dry. However, the trail can be hiked year-round, although it is advisable to avoid hiking during the winter months, when the weather can be unpredictable and dangerous.

Monte Cinto

The Monte Cinto Trail is a challenging hike that takes about 7-10 hours to complete. The trail starts at either Haut Asco or Lozzi, and follows the GR®20 route to the summit. The ascent to the ridge is extremely demanding, and requires good physical fitness and mountaineering experience. The trail follows the rocky ridge and offers spectacular views from coast to coast to the top. The descent requires the greatest caution.

The Monte Cinto Trail is a sensational course to be undertaken with the right equipment. Hikers should bring proper hiking boots, hiking poles, a backpack, sunscreen, a hat, sunglasses, and plenty of water and snacks. The weather can change rapidly in high mountains, so it is important to be prepared for all conditions.

The best time to hike the Monte Cinto Trail is during the spring or fall, when the weather is mild. The trail is also open during the summer, but hikers should be aware that the temperatures can be very hot and the conditions can be more challenging.

Corsican Waterfalls

Corsica is a beautiful island with a rugged coastline, stunning mountains, and lush forests. It is also home to some of the most spectacular waterfalls in the Mediterranean.

Here are some of the most popular waterfalls in Corsica:

- Piscia di Gallu is the tallest waterfall in Corsica, with a drop of over 60 meters. It is located in the Balagne region, near the town of Calvi. The waterfall is accessible by a short hike, and the views from the top are simply breathtaking.

- Cascades des Anglais is a series of three waterfalls located in the Restonica Valley. The waterfalls are surrounded by lush vegetation, and the water is crystal clear. The Cascades des Anglais are a popular destination for hikers and daytrippers.
- Purcaraccia is a group of waterfalls located in the Fango Valley. The waterfalls are surrounded by towering cliffs, and the water is a stunning turquoise color. Purcaraccia is a popular destination for hikers and photographers

- Cascade du Voile de la Mariée is a single waterfall located in the Restonica Valley. The waterfall is named after the way the water cascades down the cliff, resembling a bride's veil. Cascade du Voile de la Mariée is a popular destination for hikers and daytrippers.

CORSICAN CUISINE AND LOCAL DELIGHTS

Corsican Cheese and Charcuterie

- **Brocciu:** This is the most famous Corsican cheese, and it is made from the whey of sheep or goat's milk. It has a soft, creamy texture and a mild, milky flavor. Brocciu can be eaten fresh, grilled, or baked, and it is often used in traditional Corsican dishes such as fiadone and panzetta.

- **Tomme:** This is a hard cheese made from sheep or goat's milk. It has a nutty flavor and a firm texture. Tomme is often aged for several months, and it can be eaten on its own or used in cooked dishes.

- **Venachesu:** This is a blue cheese made from sheep's milk. It has a strong, pungent flavor and a crumbly texture. Venachesu is often aged for several months, and it is best eaten on its own or with crusty bread.

- **Figatellu:** This is a sausage made from pork liver and meat. It is flavored with spices, garlic, and red wine. Figatellu has a strong, distinctive flavor and a slightly chewy texture. It is traditionally grilled or roasted, and it is often served with crusty bread and a glass of red wine.

- **Coppa:** This is a cured ham made from pork shoulder. It is flavored with spices and smoked over oak wood. Coppa has a rich, smoky flavor and a firm texture. It is often served as an appetizer or as part of a charcuterie board.

- **Lonzu:** This is a cured pork loin. It is flavored with spices and salted. Lonzu has a delicate, nutty flavor and a firm texture. It is often served as an appetizer or as part of a charcuterie board.

Seafood and Fish Specialties

- **Brandade de morue.** This is a creamy codfish brandade, typically served with croutons or potatoes. It is a classic Corsican dish that is both rich and flavorful.

- **Thon grillé. Grilled tuna** is a popular dish in Corsica, and it is often served with a simple lemon and herb sauce. The tuna is fresh and flavorful, and the grill marks add a nice touch.

- **Bouillabaisse.** This is a hearty fish stew that is made with a variety of seafood, including octopus, squid, and shellfish. It is a popular dish in many Mediterranean countries, but it is said to have originated in Corsica.

Traditional Corsican Dishes

- **Civet de Sanglier:** This is arguably the signature dish of Corsica. It is a slow-cooked stew of wild boar, typically served with potatoes and onions. The boar is marinated in wine and herbs before being cooked in a rich sauce made with tomatoes, garlic, and spices. The result is a hearty and flavorful dish that is perfect for a cold winter day.

- **Veau aux Olives:** This is a delicious stew of veal that is cooked with olives, tomatoes, and herbs. The veal is typically slow-cooked in a white wine sauce, which gives it a rich and flavorful taste. The olives add a salty and briny flavor that complements the veal perfectly. This dish is often served with crusty bread to soak up the delicious juices.

- **Fiadone:** This is a traditional Corsican dessert that is made with fresh cheese, eggs, and sugar. The cheese is typically brocciu, which is a type of ricotta that is made on the island. The fiadone is baked in a tart shell and is often served with a dusting of sugar. It is a light and refreshing dessert that is perfect for after a meal.

Corsican Pastries and Desserts

- **Fiadone:** Fiadone is a traditional Corsican cheesecake made with brocciu cheese, eggs, and lemon zest. It is a light and fluffy dessert with a slightly tart flavor. Fiadone is often served with a dollop of whipped cream or a drizzle of honey.

- **Canistrelli:** Canistrelli are traditional Corsican biscuits made with flour, sugar, olive oil, and aniseed. They are crunchy on the outside and chewy on the inside. Canistrelli are often served as a snack or dessert, or they can be dipped in coffee or tea.

- **Tian:** Tian is a Corsican tart made with chestnut flour, eggs, sugar, and spices. It is a dense and flavorful tart that is often served with a scoop of ice cream or a dollop of whipped cream.

CORSICAN CULTURAL EXPERIENCES

Traditional Festivals and Celebrations

- **Fiera di U Casgiu (Cheese Festival) in Venaco:** This festival celebrates the island's traditional cheese-making methods. Visitors can sample a variety of cheeses, watch cheese-making demonstrations, and learn about the history of cheesemaking on Corsica.

- **Fiera di l'Alivu (Olive Festival) in Montegrosso:** This festival celebrates the island's olive trees and olive oil. Visitors can sample a variety of olive oils, learn about

the history of olive oil production on Corsica, and watch traditional olive oil pressing demonstrations.

- **Foire de l'Amandier (Almond Festival) in Aregno:** This festival celebrates the island's almond trees and almond products. Visitors can sample a variety of almond-based foods, learn about the history of almond production on Corsica, and watch traditional almond harvesting demonstrations.
- **Porto Latino in Saint-Florent:** This festival celebrates Latin American music and culture. Visitors can enjoy concerts by Latin American artists, dance workshops, and traditional Latin American food.

Corsican Music and Polyphonic Singing

Corsican music is a rich and diverse tradition that reflects the island's unique history and culture. The most distinctive form of Corsican music is polyphonic singing, which is characterized by its complex harmonies and improvisatory nature. Polyphonic singing is a cappella, meaning that it is sung without any instrumental accompaniment.

The origins of Corsican polyphonic singing are unclear, but it is thought to have developed in the Middle Ages. The tradition was originally practiced by men, but women began to sing polyphonically in the 19th century. Today, both men and women sing polyphonically in Corsica.

There are many different types of polyphonic songs in Corsica, including paghjelle, terzetti, madrigali, lamenti, and nanne. Paghjelle are the most common type of polyphonic song, and they are typically sung in a 4-part harmony. Terzetti are sung in a 3-part harmony, madrigali are sung in a 6-part harmony, lamenti are funeral songs, and nanne are lullabies.

Corsican polyphonic singing is a UNESCO-recognized intangible cultural heritage. The tradition has declined in recent decades, but it has seen a resurgence in popularity in recent years. There are now many active polyphonic singing groups in Corsica, and the tradition is taught in schools and music conservatories.

Corsican Language and Customs

Corsican has a long and rich history, and it was once the only language spoken on the island. However, in the 19th century, French became the official language of Corsica, and Corsican began to decline. In recent years, there has been a resurgence of interest in Corsican, and it is now taught in schools and used in government and the media.

One of the most important aspects of Corsican culture is the language, which is called Corsican (Corsu). Corsican is a Romance language that is closely related to Italian, and it is spoken by about 300,000 people on the island.

In addition to the language, there are many other aspects of Corsican culture that are unique to the island. These include the traditional Corsican costume, which is a colorful dress for women and a white shirt and black pants for men; the Corsican cuisine, which is based on fresh seafood, mountain cheeses, and olive oil; and the Corsican music, which is a mix of traditional folk songs and modern pop.

Corsican customs are also distinctive. For example, Corsicans are known for their hospitality, and they often welcome guests with a traditional Corsican meal.

They are also very proud of their island, and they often speak with a strong Corsican accent.

Corsican Craftsmanship and Souvenirs

- **Jewelry:** Corsican jewelry is made from a variety of materials, including silver, gold, and coral. The designs are often inspired by the island's natural beauty, and many pieces feature symbols of Corsica, such as the Moor's head.

- **Knives:** Corsican knives are known for

their sharp blades and beautiful handles. They are often made from local materials, such as wood and steel.

- **Pottery:** Corsican pottery is made from a type of clay that is found only on the island. The pottery is often decorated with traditional motifs, such as the Corsican flag or the Moor's head.

- **Clothing:** Corsican clothing is made from traditional fabrics, such as wool and linen. The designs are often simple and elegant, and many pieces feature traditional Corsican embroidery.

- **Food:** Corsican food is renowned for its fresh ingredients and simple flavors. Some of the most popular Corsican souvenirs include bottles of olive oil, jars of chestnut jam, and wheels of brocciu cheese.

Corsican Museums

- **Musée Fesch in Ajaccio:** This museum is home to one of the most important collections of Italian Renaissance art outside of Italy. The collection was assembled by Cardinal Joseph Fesch, Napoleon's uncle, and includes works by Botticelli, Raphael, Titian, and Caravaggio.

- **Maison Bonaparte in Ajaccio:** This is the birthplace of Napoleon Bonaparte, and the museum tells the story of his life and his family. The house is furnished in the style of the 18th century, and it contains many personal belongings of Napoleon and his family.

- **Musée de la Corse in Corte:** This museum is dedicated to the history and culture of Corsica. It houses a collection of archaeological artifacts, ethnographic objects, and works of art. The museum also offers a variety of temporary exhibitions.

- **Musée d'Archéologie d'Aléria in Aléria:** This museum is located in the ancient city of Aléria, which was founded by the Romans in the 3rd century BC. The museum houses a collection of archaeological artifacts from the site, including pottery, jewelry, and coins.

OUTDOOR ACTIVITIES IN CORSICA

Hiking and Trekking

One of the most popular hikes in Corsica is the GR20. This long-distance trail runs from Calenzana in the west to Conca in the east, and is considered to be one of the toughest hikes in Europe. The GR20 is a challenging hike, but the rewards are great. Along the way, hikers will enjoy stunning views of the mountains, forests, and valleys.

If you're looking for a shorter hike, there are plenty of other options available.

The Capo Rosso hike is a great choice for those who want to enjoy the beauty of the Calanques de Piana. The Cascades de Purcaraccia hike is a fun and challenging hike that takes hikers through a beautiful waterfall gorge. And the Source des Roches Bleues hike is a peaceful hike that leads to a beautiful blue lake.

Watersports and Sailing

- **Sailing:** Corsica is a popular destination for sailing, thanks to its mild climate and protected waters. There are many different sailing schools and charter companies on the island, so you can learn to sail or take a boat out for a day trip.

- **Windsurfing:** Windsurfing is another popular watersport in Corsica, thanks to the strong winds that blow along the coast. There are many different spots to windsurf on the island, from beginner-friendly beaches to more challenging spots for experienced windsurfers.

- **Kitesurfing:** Kitesurfing is a relatively new watersport that is becoming increasingly popular in Corsica.

Kitesurfers use a large kite to harness the power of the wind and propel themselves across the water.

- Kayaking: Kayaking is a great way to explore the coastline of Corsica. There are many different kayaking tours available, from short trips around the bays to longer expeditions into the mountains.

- Stand-up paddleboarding: Stand-up paddleboarding is a relatively new watersport that is becoming increasingly popular in Corsica. Stand-up

paddleboarders use a long paddle to propel themselves across the water.

- Snorkeling and scuba diving: Corsica's clear waters offer some of the best snorkeling and scuba diving in the Mediterranean. There are many different dive sites to choose from, including wrecks, caves, and reefs.

Canyoning and Rafting

rivers in Corsica are also well-suited for rafting, and there are a number of companies that offer guided tours.

Canyoning

Canyoning is an adventure sport that involves exploring a river canyon by jumping, swimming, rappelling, and sliding down natural waterslides. It is a great way to experience the natural beauty of Corsica, and it is also a lot of fun.

The island has a number of canyons that offer a variety of challenges, from easy beginner trails to more challenging descents. The

Some of the best canyons for canyoning in Corsica include:

● **The Pulischellu Canyon:** This is a

popular canyon for beginners, and it offers a variety of activities, including jumping, swimming, and rappelling.

- **The Vacca Canyon**: This is a more challenging canyon, and it offers some exciting rappels and jumps.
- **The Purcaraccia Canyon**: This is a beautiful canyon with stunning waterfalls, and it is a great place to go canyoning if you are looking for a challenge.

Rafting

Rafting is another great way to experience the rivers of Corsica. It is a fun and exhilarating activity that is suitable for people of all ages.

Some of the best rivers for rafting in Corsica include:

- **The Tavignano River**: This is a popular river for rafting, and it offers a variety of rapids, from easy to challenging.
- **The Fango River**: This is a more challenging

river, and it offers some exciting rapids.

- The Rizzanese River: This is a beautiful river with stunning scenery, and it is a great place to go rafting if you are looking for a more relaxed experience.

Rock Climbing and Via Ferrata

Rock Climbing

Corsica has a long history of rock climbing, and there are many well-established routes to choose from. The most popular areas for rock climbing include the Calanques de Piana, the Gulf of Porto, and the Bavella Massif. These areas offer a variety of climbs, from easy to difficult, and are suitable for both beginners and experienced climbers.

Via Ferrata

- Via ferrata is a type of mountaineering that combines elements of rock climbing and hiking. Via ferrata routes are equipped with cables, ladders, and other aids to help climbers ascend steep terrain. This makes via ferrata a more accessible activity than traditional rock climbing, and it is a great way to experience the thrill of climbing without the need for extensive technical skills.

Cycling and Mountain Biking

For road cyclists, there are challenging climbs and long-distance routes that wind through forests, past vineyards, and along the coast. The GR20, a long-distance hiking trail that crosses the island from north to south, is also popular with cyclists.

Mountain bikers will find plenty of challenging trails to explore, from singletrack trails in the mountains to more technical trails in the forests. Some of the most popular mountain biking areas include the Aiguilles de Bavella, the Désert des

Agriates, and the Asco Valley.

- **Aiguilles de Bavella:** This mountain range in the south of Corsica is home to some of the most challenging and technical mountain biking trails on the island.
- **Désert des Agriates:** This remote desert in the north of Corsica is a great place to find challenging road cycling climbs and scenic singletrack trails.
- **Asco Valley:** This valley in the centre of Corsica is home to a variety of mountain biking trails, from easy to challenging.
- **Cap Corse:** This peninsula in the north of Corsica offers stunning coastal views and challenging road cycling climbs.
- **Calvi:** This town in the north of Corsica is a popular base for cyclists and mountain bikers, with a variety of trails to choose from.

CORSICAN TOWNS AND VILLAGES

Sartène

The town is built on a hilltop, and its old town is surrounded by imposing walls. The streets of the old town are narrow and winding, and they are lined with traditional Corsican houses. There are several churches in the old town, including the Cathédrale de l'Assomption, which was built in the 16th century.

Sartène is also home to a number of museums, including the Musée d'Archéologie et d'Ethnographie de la Corse, which houses a collection of artifacts from the island's history. There is also a museum dedicated to the Corsican painter Jean-Baptiste Rossi.

Outside of the old town, there are a number of things to see and do in Sartène. There are several beaches within a short drive of the town, including the beaches of Saleccia and Palombaggia. There are also opportunities for hiking, biking, and fishing in the surrounding area.

Here are some of the things you can experience in Sartène:

- Explore the old town's narrow streets and admire the traditional Corsican architecture.
- Visit the Cathédrale de l'Assomption and learn about the island's history.
- Visit the Musée d'Archéologie et d'Ethnographie de la Corse and see artifacts from the island's past.
- Visit the Musée Jean-Baptiste Rossi and learn about the work of this famous Corsican painter.
- Relax on one of the beautiful beaches

nearby, such as Saleccia or Palombaggia.

- Go hiking, biking, or fishing in the surrounding countryside.
- Sample the local cuisine, which features traditional Corsican dishes such as pâté de sanglier (wild boar sausage) and figatellu (black sausage).
- Attend one of the town's festivals, such as the Sartène Historical Festival or the Sartène Jazz Festival.

Nonza

It is known for its stunning location, with houses perched on cliffs overlooking the sea. The village is also home to a number of historical sites, including a 16th-century church, a Genoese tower, and the ruins of an old castle.

One of the best things to do in Nonza is to simply wander around the village and take in the views. The narrow streets are lined with traditional Corsican houses, and there are a number of viewpoints where you can get stunning panoramic views of the coast.

If you're looking for something a little more

active, there are a number of hiking trails in the area. You can hike to the top of the cliffs for even more amazing views, or take a walk along the coast to the beach.

The beach in Nonza is a small black sand beach, which is a bit unusual for Corsica. The beach is not suitable for swimming, but it is a great place to sunbathe or just relax and enjoy the scenery.

Here are some other things to experience in Nonza:

- Visit the 16th-century church of Saint Julie.
- Climb the Genoese tower for panoramic

views of the village and the coast.

- Explore the ruins of the old castle.
- Hike to the top of the cliffs for even more amazing views.
- Take a walk along the coast to the beach.
- Visit one of the small restaurants in the village and sample traditional Corsican cuisine.
- Enjoy a drink at one of the bars in the village and watch the sunset over the sea.

Corte

Corte is a town in the north of Corsica, and it is the former capital of the island.

It is a beautiful town, set in a dramatic setting at the foot of the Monte Renoso mountains. Corte is a popular tourist destination, and it is known for its rich history, its stunning scenery, and its vibrant cultural scene. *There are many things to see and do in Corte. Some of the most popular attractions include:*

- **The Citadel:** The Citadel is a massive fortress that dominates the town of Corte. It was built in the 15th century, and it has been used as a military base, a prison, and a royal palace.

- **The Museum of Corsica:** The Museum of Corsica is a great place to learn about the history and culture of

the island. The museum has exhibits on everything from prehistory to the Napoleonic era.

- **The Botanical Garden:** The Botanical Garden is a beautiful garden located in the heart of Corte. It is home to a wide variety of plants, including many endemic species.
- **The Gorges de la Restonica:** The Gorges de la Restonica are a stunning natural wonder located just outside of Corte. The gorges are a popular destination for hiking, swimming, and canyoning.

Calvi Citadel

The citadel was built in the 14th century by the Republic of Genoa, and has been well-preserved over the centuries. The walls of the citadel are over 20 meters high, and there are several towers and bastions that offer stunning views of the surrounding area. Inside the citadel, there are narrow streets, charming squares, and a number of historical buildings, including the 15th century cathedral, the Governor's Palace, and the Citadel Museum.

There are a number of things to experience in Calvi Citadel. You can wander around the narrow streets and admire the architecture, visit the cathedral or the Citadel Museum, or take in the stunning views from the ramparts. There are also a number of restaurants and cafes in the citadel, where you can enjoy a meal or a drink with a view.

If you are looking for something more active, you can go for a walk or hike around the citadel walls, or visit the nearby beaches. There are also a number of boat tours that depart from Calvi, which offer the opportunity to see the citadel from the sea.

Here are some additional things to experience in Calvi Citadel:

- Visit the Citadelle Museum, which houses a collection of artifacts from the history of Calvi.
- Take a walk or hike around the ramparts of the citadel, and enjoy the stunning views of the surrounding area.
- Visit the nearby beaches, such as Calvi Beach or Algajola Beach.
- Take a boat tour of the Gulf of Calvi, and see the citadel from the sea.
- Enjoy a meal or a drink at one of the many restaurants or cafes in the citadel.
- Attend one of the many festivals or events that are held in Calvi throughout the year.

Saint-Florent

It is situated in the Gulf of Saint-Florent, which is sheltered by the mountains of Cap Corse and the Désert des Agriates. The town has a long history, dating back to the Roman period. It was later a flourishing medieval port under the rule of Genoa. Today, Saint-Florent is a popular tourist destination, known for its charming old town, beautiful beaches, and stunning scenery.

What to experience in Saint-Florent

- **Explore the old town:** The old town of Saint-Florent is a UNESCO World Heritage Site. It is a maze of narrow streets and alleyways, lined with shops, restaurants, and cafes. There are also several historical buildings in the old town, including the Genoese citadel, the church of Saint-Florent, and the town hall.

- **Visit the beaches:** Saint-Florent is surrounded by some of the most beautiful beaches in Corsica. The most popular beaches include the Plage de la Roya, the Plage de Saleccia, and the Plage de Loto.
- **Go hiking:** There are several hiking trails in the area around Saint-Florent. One popular trail is the Sentier des Douaniers, which follows the coastline from Saint-Florent to the Désert des Agriates.
- **Take a boat trip:** There are several boat trips available from Saint-Florent. You can take a boat trip to the Lavezzi Islands, the Île de Beauté, or the Désert des Agriates.

- **Enjoy the nightlife:** Saint-Florent has a lively nightlife scene. There are several bars and clubs in the town, where you can enjoy drinks, dancing, and live music.

Pigna

The village has a long history, dating back to the 9th century. It was originally founded by a group of monks who built a monastery here. The monastery was destroyed by the Saracens in the 10th century, but the village survived and continued to grow.

Pigna is a popular tourist destination, and for good reason. The village is absolutely beautiful, and there are plenty of things to see and do here. Here are a few of the things you can experience in Pigna:

- **Explore the village's narrow streets and admire the traditional architecture.** The village is a maze of narrow streets and alleyways, lined with brightly colored houses. Take your time wandering through the village, and be sure to stop to admire the architecture. Some of the houses date back to the 16th century, and they are beautifully preserved.

- **Visit the church of Saint-Pancrace.** The church of Saint-Pancrace is the oldest building in Pigna. It was built in the 12th century, and it is a beautiful example of Romanesque architecture. The church is worth visiting for its architecture, as well as for its stunning views of the surrounding countryside.

- **Enjoy the views from the Belvedere.** The Belvedere is a viewpoint located at the top of the village. It offers stunning views of the surrounding countryside, including the Mediterranean Sea. The Belvedere is a great place to relax and enjoy the views.

- **Visit the Pigna Music Festival.** The Pigna Music Festival is a annual festival that takes place in July. The festival features a variety of traditional Corsican music, as well as other genres of music. The festival is a great way to experience Corsican culture and enjoy some good music.

Algajola

There are many things to experience in Algajola. Visitors can relax on the town's long sandy beach, swim in the clear blue waters of the Mediterranean Sea, or go for a walk or bike ride along the waterfront promenade. The town also has a number of historical sites, including the 16th-century Genoese fort, the ruins of a Roman villa, and the Church of Saint-Michel.

In addition to its natural beauty and historical attractions, Algajola also has a vibrant cultural scene. There are a number of art galleries and museums in the town, as well as a number of restaurants and bars where visitors can enjoy traditional Corsican cuisine.

Here are some of the specific things you can experience in Algajola:

- **Relax on the beach:** Algajola's long sandy beach is one of the town's most popular attractions. The beach is sheltered from the wind, making it a great place to relax and soak up the sun.

- **Go swimming:** The waters off Algajola are clear and warm, making them perfect for swimming. You can also go snorkeling or diving to explore the underwater world.

- **Visit the Genoese fort:** The Genoese fort was built in the 16th century and offers stunning views of the town and the surrounding area. You can walk around the fort and explore its ramparts.

- **Explore the old town:** Algajola's old town is a charming maze of narrow streets and alleyways. There are a number of shops, cafes, and restaurants in the old town, as well as a few historical sites.

Erbalunga

It is situated on a rocky promontory, with a Genoese tower overlooking the harbor. The village is a popular tourist destination, thanks to its beautiful setting, its historical attractions, and its lively atmosphere.

Here are some of the things you can experience in Erbalunga:

- **Explore the village's narrow streets and alleyways.** Erbalunga is a small village, but it is packed with character. The streets are lined with traditional Corsican houses, and there are plenty of hidden corners to discover.

- **Visit the Genoese tower.** The Genoese tower is the most iconic landmark in Erbalunga. It was built in the 16th century, and it offers stunning views of the village and the surrounding coastline.

- **Stroll along the harbor.** The harbor is the heart of Erbalunga. It is a lively place, with fishing boats bobbing in the water and people enjoying the sunshine. There are also a few cafes and restaurants along the harbor, where you can enjoy a drink or a meal with a view.

- **Sample the local cuisine.** Erbalunga is a great place to sample traditional Corsican cuisine. There are a number of excellent restaurants in the village, where you can enjoy dishes such as grilled fish, pasta, and pastries.

.

- **Attend the Jazz Festival.** Every August, Erbalunga hosts a jazz festival. The festival features a variety of local and international musicians, and it is a great opportunity to enjoy some live music in a beautiful setting

Olmeto

One of the main attractions in Olmeto is its old town. The narrow streets are lined with traditional Corsican houses, many of which date back to the 17th and 18th centuries. There are also several churches and chapels in the old town, including the 16th-century Church of Santa Maria, which is worth a visit for its beautiful Baroque architecture.

Another popular attraction in Olmeto is its beaches. The most popular beach is Olmeto-Beach, which is a long stretch of sandy beach with clear blue waters. There are also several smaller beaches in the area, including Cala di Conca, which is a secluded cove with crystal-clear waters.

In addition to its beaches and historical attractions,

place in July. There are also several museums in Olmeto, including the Museum of Corsican Ethnography, which tells the story of the island's culture and history.

Here are some of the things you can experience in Olmeto:

- Explore the old town's narrow streets and admire the traditional Corsican architecture.
- Visit the Church of Santa Maria and admire its Baroque interior.
- Relax on one of the beautiful beaches, such as Olmeto-Beach or Cala di Conca.
- Hike or bike in the surrounding hills.

Olmeto also has a vibrant cultural life. There are several festivals held in the village throughout the year, including the Corsican Music Festival, which takes

- Visit the Museum of Corsican Ethnography and learn about the island's culture and history.

- Attend one of the many festivals held in the village throughout the year.

Porto

The beaches in Porto are some of the best in Corsica. They are long, sandy, and backed by pine trees. The water is clear and blue, and the swimming is excellent. Some of the most popular beaches in Porto include Palombaggia, Santa Giulia, and Plage de Ficajola.

The old town of Porto is a charming maze of narrow streets and colorful houses. There are many shops, cafes, and restaurants in the old town, and it is a great place to wander around and explore. The highlight of the old town is the Citadelle, a medieval fortress that offers stunning views of the surrounding area.

In addition to its beaches and its old town, Porto also has a number of other things to offer visitors. There are several hiking trails in the surrounding area, and there are also opportunities for fishing, sailing, and windsurfing. Porto is also a popular destination for birdwatching, as there are many species of birds that can be seen in the area.

Here are some of the things you can experience in Porto:

- Visit the Citadelle, a medieval fortress that offers stunning views of the surrounding area.
- Explore the old town, a charming maze of

narrow streets and colorful houses.

- Relax on one of the beautiful beaches, such as Palombaggia, Santa Giulia, or Plage de Ficajola.
- Go hiking in the surrounding hills.
- Go fishing, sailing, or windsurfing.
- Go birdwatching, as there are many species of birds that can be seen in the area.
- Enjoy the lively atmosphere of Porto, with its many shops, cafes, and restaurants.

PRACTICAL INFORMATION AND TIPS

Transportation in Corsica

- **Ferry:** Ferries are the most common way to get to Corsica, and there are routes from France, Italy, and even Tunisia. The cost of a ferry ticket will vary depending on the time of year and the port of departure, but you can expect to pay around €70-220 for a standard car and driver.
- **Train:** There is a train line that runs along the east coast of Corsica, connecting Bastia, Ajaccio, and Calvi. Tickets are relatively inexpensive, starting at around €10 for a single journey.

- **Bus:** There are a number of bus companies that operate in Corsica, providing services to most of the major towns and villages. Buses are a good option for budget travelers, with tickets starting at around €5 for a single journey.

- **Car rental:** If you want to have the freedom to explore Corsica at your own pace, then renting a car is a good option. Car rental prices vary depending on the season and the type of car you choose, but you can expect to pay around €35 per day for a small car.

- **Taxi:** Taxis are a convenient way to get around, but they can be expensive. A taxi ride from Bastia to Ajaccio will cost around €150.

Safety and Emergency Contacts

some safety tips for tourists in Corsica:

- Be aware of your surroundings. This is especially important in crowded areas, such as tourist hotspots or public transportation. Keep your belongings close to you and don't flash expensive jewelry or electronics.
- Don't walk alone at night. If you must walk alone at night, stick to well-lit areas and avoid secluded streets.
- Be careful when swimming. The currents in the Mediterranean can be strong, so be

Corsica is a relatively safe destination for tourists, but it is always a good idea to be aware of your surroundings and take some basic precautions. Here are sure to swim in designated areas and never swim alone.

- Be aware of the wildlife. There are some venomous snakes and spiders in Corsica, so be careful when hiking or camping.
- Carry your passport and emergency contact information with you at all times.

Here are some emergency contacts in Corsica:

- Police: 17
- Fire department: 18
- Medical emergency: 112
- Tourist information: 0811 226 226

If you need to report a crime, you can call the police on 17. If there is a fire, call the fire department on 18. For a medical emergency, call 112. You can also call the tourist information number, 0811 226 226, for help with anything from finding your way around to reporting a crime.

Currency and Money Matters

Currency in Corsica

- The currency of Corsica is the euro (EUR). One euro is divided into 100 cents. Euros are available in both coins and notes.

Credit Cards

- Credit cards are widely accepted in Corsica, especially in the larger towns and tourist resorts. However, it is always a good idea to have some cash on hand, as there may be some places that do not accept credit cards.

Exchanging Currency

- You can exchange currency at banks, currency exchange bureaus, and some hotels. The best exchange rates are usually found at banks, but they may have shorter opening hours than currency exchange bureaus.

Traveler's Checks

- Traveler's checks are not as widely accepted in Corsica as they used to be. However, they can still be exchanged at banks and some currency exchange bureaus.

ATMs

- There are ATMs in most towns and tourist resorts in Corsica. You can use your ATM card to withdraw cash from your bank account in euros.

Tips

- If you are planning on using your credit card in Corsica, make sure that it has a chip and PIN. Chip and PIN technology is widely used in France, and some merchants may not accept cards without a chip.
- If you are exchanging currency, do your research to find the best exchange rate. You can compare exchange rates online or ask your hotel or tour operator for recommendations.
- Keep a small amount of cash in your wallet for small purchases. This will save you from having to pay ATM fees every time you need cash.

Useful Phrases and Etiquette

Phrases

- Hello: Bongiorno (in the morning) or Bonsoir (in the evening)
- Goodbye: Arrivederci
- Please: Per favore
- Thank you: Grazie

- You're welcome: Prego
- Excuse me: Scusi
- Do you speak English?: Parla inglese?
- I don't speak French: Non parlo francese
- How much does this cost?: Quanto costa?
- I would like...: Vorrei...
- I'm full: Sono sazio
- I'm thirsty: Ho sete
- I'm tired: Sono stanco

Etiquette

- Corsicans are a proud people, so it's important to be respectful of their culture.
- When you're invited to someone's home, it's customary to bring a gift, such as a bottle of wine or flowers.
- Tipping is not expected in Corsica, but it is appreciated.
- When you're dining in a restaurant, it's customary to order aperitifs, main courses, and desserts.
- It's considered rude to leave food on your plate.
- When you're finished eating, you should leave the table clean.

Other tips

- If you're planning on hiking or camping, be sure to be prepared for the elements.

- Corsicans are very proud of their language, so it's a nice gesture to learn a few basic phrases.
- If you're driving in Corsica, be aware that the speed limit is much lower than in other parts of Europe.
- Be sure to try the local cuisine, which is known for its fresh seafood and pasta dishes.

Printed in Great Britain
by Amazon

26283888R00057